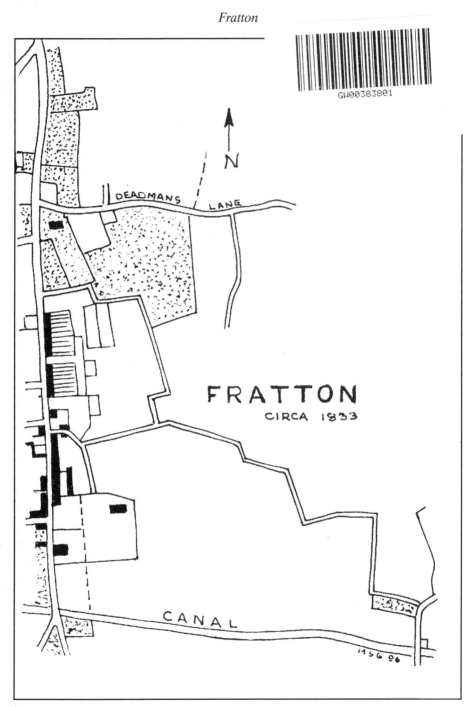

Fratton 1833

Fratton

Fratton Road is the subject of this latest booklet in our series of memories of Portsmouth.

Fratton Road is part of one of the old lanes that ran roughly north-south across the island through the fields. The lane has since been straightened, widened and split into sections. It was the lane that led through the island to the manor of Froddington after which it takes its name, Fratton being a corruption of Froddington. The manor lay to the south of Fratton Bridge where the lane split in two, even before the canal and later the railway came to the town.

Trams in Fratton

In 1882 the Fratton & Southsea Tramway Company proposed a line from Kingston to Southsea, commencing at Powerscourt Road, Kingston where there was a horse tram stable, and running through Fratton Road to South Parade Pier. The section from Kingston to Fratton Bridge was opened on 22 February 1886. In 1892 the company was sold to Provincial Tramways which was later bought by the Corporation.

In August 1927, the tramways committee agreed to relay the tracks in Fratton Road from Kingston Cross to Fratton Bridge. The Council tried to overrule this but failed and work started in 1928. Between St. Mary's Church and Fratton Road the east side of the road was set back and many buildings demolished or rebuilt. The track was relaid as double and opened on 25th July 1929 by the Lord Mayor. The new trolley buses started running through Fratton in 1933.

We have used the 1934 Kelly's directory as a basis for the business premises in the roads in the area.

Adames Road, named after B.Adames, Chichester councillor who chaired railway development meetings. The northern part was earlier called Hanover Street after the Royal house.

East Side

1	Frank Fulford, Beer Retailer
	Was on the corner with St. Mary's Road and is first listed in 1887 as the Royal Oak. Later it is only listed as a beer retailer last listed in 1946.
45-47	Mrs Annie Redman, Beer Retailer
	The Windsor Castle, off licence. It is listed from 1898 to 1976 as a beer retailer.
	The building has now been converted into two houses.
63	Edwin Prin, Greengrocer

West Side

2-4	T.E.Layton & Sons, Truck Lenders
38	Alfred Green, Bootmaker

At the end of the road are some old stables

Alver Road, was originally named Alva Road and was built in 1860.

South Side

10	Harry Short, Greengrocer
26	William Gapper, Shopkeeper
60	Arthur Lloyd, Insurance Agent
92	James Knight, Cycle Dealer

One property on the south side is unusual and could be an old farm building.

North Side

Just inside the churchyard were for many years some public conveniences.

1a	Buckingham Bros, Monumental Mason (1934 to 1958) it became Alver-Stones, Monumental Masons (1962 to 1976)

Although the name has changed, the business is still in the family, Buckingham being the maiden name of the grandmother of the present owner.

Ariel Road

In 1887 the listing is Charles Day, Market Gardener at Speck's Farm that gave its name to the lane from Fratton to Milton.

West Side
    28   Miss E Rose Brockway, Costumier
East Side
    21   John Sainsbury, Fried Fish Shop

Barnes Road, named after Robert Barnes who became Mayor, 1892. It is listed as a new estate in the 1887 directory.
East Side
    18   Edmund Martin, Boot Maker
    30   Miss Alma Griffin, Dressmaker

Brookfield Road, possibly named after Rev G.H.Brookfield. Like Barnes Road it is listed as a new estate in the 1887 directory.
South Side
    2   William Barnard, Shopkeeper
    28   Brookfield Hall

1890	St. Marys Gymnasium
1892	Transferred to St. Boniface
1898 to 1901	Mission Hall
1923 to 1928	Brookfield Mission Hall
1937 to 1938	Brookfield Mission Hall (Baptist)
1940 to 1976	Brookfield Hall (Bretheren)
1996	Brookfield Mission Hall

August 1989 Hut at back renovated to be used as Sunday School
    38   Mrs Ada Scott, Shopkeeper
    40   Harold Pratt, Grocer
North Side
    1-3   The Lord Clive, Frederick Isaccson
               First listed in 1891 as a public house at 3 Brookfield Road. It may date from 1887 when 77 Guildford Road is listed as Lord Clyde. Named from 1898 directory onward. Closed in 1977 the building was converted into flats. It was originally a Goodman's house.
    17   Pope Bros, Bakers (1928 to 1956) later Grenfield Ltd., Bakers (1958 to 1960).By 1962 the premises were in use by a cabinet maker, Grenfields having moved to Trafalgar Place as Builders and Joiners. The site is now occupied by housing.
               "My father used to work for Pope Bros, wholesale bakery. They were in business before Sept 1926 when my parents were married and Dad was employed to deliver as well as bake. He used to travel around in an old Dunalt motor bike and sidecar to Gosport, Fareham and other areas around locally. Between 1926 and 1928 they had a shop in New Road selling pies, cakes and

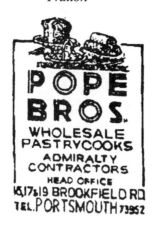

buns to the Dockyardsmen on their way to work or home. The shop where my mother worked was later taken over by a relation of Mr Popes.

The bakehouse I remember well, the entrance in Moorland Road faced straight onto some very steep wooden stairs up to the flour loft. To the left of the entrance was a store room where the glace cherries were stored and shortcakes that were accidentally broken were also put. I used to enjoy some of both on my visits with Dad. He used to cycle there on Sunday morning or afternoon to check the coke ovens that were drawn, relit and banked up ready for an early start on Monday morning - 4am. I can still smell the sharp hot coke fumes and hear the crickets singing under the ovens. Working with Dad, Christian name Frank, but known to everybody as Eric were the Kilner brothers, John, Harry and 'Dink' who I believe lived with their mother next-door in Brookfield Road. Later during the war and after 'Big Jo', 'Little Jo' and Vi, John's wife also worked there. During the war John and his wife ran a standby bakehouse at Wickham which was Quintins and is now the Post Office. There I met my wife who was working there when Dad stood in for John for a fortnight."

Keith Barnard

19   Mrs A Tidy, Shopkeeper

"The usual shop of the time selling everything from bread to shoelaces."

Byerley Road

In the 1887 directory this is listed as a new estate with two terraces of houses Shelbert Terrace and Byerley Terrace.

East Side
41	Edgar Fletcher, Slater
59	Listed from 1898 to 1902 as Aylesbury Dairy, J.W.Moore

This became a builders then a garage. Currently it is Byerley Road Garage run by Mr Bunguard.

between 59 & 61 was Railway Cottage, now demolished.

143	Miss E Simmonds, Shopkeeper

West Side
66	Albert Powell & Son, Confectioners. The shop stayed in the family becoming a grocery shop by 1971.

Simmond's Beer Shop

90-92	Ernest Simmonds, Beer Retailer

Listed as beer retailer or off licence from (1898 to 1976) It closed and was converted into two houses in 1978.

Claremont Road, was originally Claremont Terrace. Named after Prince Leopold of Claremont

West Side
9	Mrs S.Maguire, Apartments
43	Mrs V.Maslin, Apartments
57	R.L.Evelyn Ltd, Wholesale Stationers, Yard

East Side
    Hall
        1923 to 1938 Evangelical Mission Hall
    Hall

        1928 to 1958 Society of Friends meeting house
        1960 to 1967 Assembly of God, Calvary Church, Pentecostal
        1971 to 1976 Evangelical Free Church

    Fratton Railway Hotel
        1887 Rebuilt architect A.E.Cogswell for Lush's brewery.
        1911 Leased to Portsmouth United Breweries.
        From 1977 to 1982 known as the Railway Hotel.
        It has been closed for some years. It was used as a meeting place
        for a folk club for many years.
    Charles Welton, Government Contractor, Yard
    28   Miss E.Beves M.I.C.T.C.L., Teacher of Music
    36   Miss Emily Jenkins, Dressmaker

Clarkes Road
West Side
    15   Simpson & Co., Fish & Meat Paste Manufacturers
East Side
    2   Mrs F.Voller, Shopkeeper
    24   Mrs F.Voller, Shopkeeper
    Park Keepers Cottage
        Built in 1890 in Dutch style, it is now used as a nursery school,
        note the windows in the chimney.

Clive Road, named after Lord Clive.
In the 1887 directory is listed as now building and reference to two terraces
Belmont and Clive Terraces.
North Side
    1   Frank Harris, Furniture Dealer
    5   The Kingston Charging Depot & Works, accumulator charging
    5-7   Jeram & Co., Coal Merchants
        Hamilton House now occupies the site.
    5A   Portsmouth Labour Party (Headquarters)
        They met in rooms above Jeram's. Later Bob Woolgar used the
        rooms for his gym.
    9   Ronald Walker, Insurance Agent
    15   Ernest Cains, Shopkeeper
    17   Mrs Clementine Daish, Shopkeeper

35	John Campbell, Hairdresser
69A	Edward West, Shopkeeper
105	Portsmouth Labour Home, C.E.T.S. from 1898 to 1923
	Later William Sweet, Hairdresser from 1928
	"On the corner of Adames Road and Clive Road was a building that used to be the labour exchange."
107	Samuel Hedger, Boot maker
	Still a boot repairer in 1996 with Ken Burgess who has been here for sixteen years.
111	Mrs Jane Tee, Shopkeeper
115	Miss G Tuck I.U.M.T.C.L., Teacher of Music

South Side

2	Was the Trafalgar Dairy with William Shepherd from 1887 to 1902and Charles Shepherd, Dairyman from 1923 to 1951. Now a printers.
8	William Cook, Tailor
22	Mrs Mary Greenaway, Nurse
44	Miss E.Harley, I.U.M.T.C.L, Teacher of Music
64	Alfred Wells, Insurance Agent

St. Boniface Church

On 18 July 1892 the memorial stone was laid by the Duke of Connaught. It was built as a chapel of ease to St. Mary. The architect was J.H.Ball. The church was damaged on 10 Jan 1941. The church was repaired and used until 31 Dec. 1961 when it was sold to the Clive Road meeting room trust. Under their care it survived until 1972 when the church closed and was demolished. "On special Sundays we used to march round to St. Mary's Church, opposite was St. Mary's Institution where we had prize giving."

66	George Harris, Shopkeeper
82	Edward Silk, Pianoforte Tuner
88	Miss J.Maidment, Shopkeeper
110	Miss Ivy Hall, A.T.C.L., Teacher of Music
114	George Harris, Gramophone Repairer
142	Harry Shier, Grocer
	Still a grocers in 1976 but subsequently converted into a house.
194	Sidney Hales, Shopkeeper
	Still a shop in 1996 - 'Sell Alls' run by Mr & Mrs Ken Cwym who have been here for twenty-six years.

Cornwall Road, Albert Street was the earlier name of the western part of the road.

North Side

15	Putman Bros, Boot Repairer

29	Leonard Griffin, Shopkeeper
31	King & Milne, Decorators
	Now two flats and Bleach, Joiners.
41	Alfred Derrick, Dairyman

West Side

| 2 | Charles Turner, Shopkeeper |
| 50 | Miss L.Kellaway, Teacher of Music |

Cuthbert Road, possibly named after Mayor Rev George Cuthbert. Lansdown Street was the earlier name of the northern part of the street. In the 1887 directory is listed as St. Cuthbert Road.

East Side

7   James Moore, Dairyman. The Moore family were here and in Byerley Road for many years.
"My father used to work for them and at Christmas used to get drunk on the round as everyone gave him a drink."

9   Harold Rosher, Beer Retailer, Off Licence
Listed as an off licence or beer retailer from 1898 to 1958
Has been derelict for many years but recently (Feb. 1996) was gutted

35   Charles Clements, Apartments

West Side

22   Mrs L.Gadd, Shopkeeper

58   Joseph Dudley, Fried Fish Shop has since been converted into a house.

90   Henry Thomas, Grocer. The business had been in the family since 1898 when they were listed as Bakers. Now a house.

Dorset Street

On 23 September 1910 a licence was granted for the Bijou Theatre, cinema in Dorset Street. It closed by 9 January 1916.

Forton Road

North Side

1   Charles Ellis, Furniture Remover

Fratton Road

Started at Sydenham Terrace

"One of the characters of the area was the point duty policeman on Fratton Bridge, named Duchy Holland. When the hordes of Dockyard mateys were on their way home to lunch by cycle he would favour them coming out of Sydenham Terrace rather than the Fratton Road traffic stream."

On the west side, at Fratton Bridge and travelling north were:

1   Fratton Hotel, Landlord Thomas Millgate
         First listed in the trade directories in 1865 as The Queen's Head.
         It was rebuilt in 1899 to designs of local architect Vernon Inkpen
         and was renamed the Fratton Hotel. It stood on the corner until
         it was bombed in 1941 and was a Miles Brewery house.

3   Robert Welch, Restaurant
         In 1973 was still a restaurant, the Black Cat. The premises from
         here to Lucknow Street have since been demolished and the
         Royal British Legion Club now occupies the site.

5   Mrs M Stonham, Butcher

7   Mrs D Knight, Confectioner

9   Ernest King, Newsagent, bookseller, stationer and tobacconist
         "I worked there when I was twelve delivering newspapers for 4/-
         (20p) a week - a good wage in those days."

11   Ernest Bishop, dentist
         He was upstairs with an entrance in Lucknow Street.

here is Lucknow Street named after the Indian town. Lucknow became part of the
British Empire in 1856 but was seized by Indian soldiers in 1857. The British Forces
were trapped until being rescued by a British Relief Expedition in 1858.

13 to 35 were Clyde Terrace.

13   Arthur Brookman, Draper
         "Another well-known business was Brookman's on the corner of
         Lucknow Street. They sold everything in drapery and you could
         pay weekly."

15   Mrs G Graham, Music Warehouse

17   F Barnett & Sons Ltd., Fish Caterers, registered office
         "The business was actually started by the wife of Frank Barnett,
         towards the end of the 1914-1918 World War, when he was
         finding it difficult to make a living, transporting sand and shingle
         in his sailing barges. The shop, I believe, was in Somers Road, but
         later transferred to Fawcett Road. Two daughters, their
         youngest son and daughter-in-law helped her.
         When the Great War ended, and the family was again united, the
         business was expanded, to employ the sons who had been away in
         the forces. Shops were opened in various parts of the town, and
         by 1923, in addition to the above address there were also shops in
         Fawcett Road (now 2), Kingston Road, Somers Road (again)
         and Arundel Street (this was open only a short time).
         The company of F. Barnett & Sons, Limited. Fish Caterers, was
         formed in March 1928, the chairman being Frank senior. The
         directors were his sons Frank jnr., George, William, Harold,

Edward, and son-in-law George Pafford. Also in 1928 the shop in Somers Road was closed and a second shop opened in Kingston Road. At this time the registered office of the company was at the home of Frank sen., but when he retired completely in 1934, 17 Fratton Road became the registered office. Three more shops were opened in 1934, they were in Chichester Road, Locksway Road, and Tangier Road, the latter selling fresh fish by day, and fried fish and chips at night. 107 Kingston Road was closed and sold to Hoopers the ironmonger and tool merchant, when the shop that is now Haskers was built.

Things became difficult after the outbreak of World War 2, and by 1940 George and William had been directed to war work, and Harold, who had been on the Reserve of Officers since 1921, was recalled to serve as a Captain in the Royal Artillery, Coast Defence. This left only Frank jnr. and George Pafford to manage with reduced supplies, so Fratton Road, Fawcett Road and Kingston Road were closed for the duration of the war.

Edward left the firm some while before the war started, George and William did not return to the business after the war either, so Frank, Harold when he returned, and George Pafford continued with Tangier Road and Milton Road selling fresh fish, Chichester Road frying, the remaining shops were sold or leased and continued to supply fish and chips for a long time after. When George Pafford retired in 1946 Chichester Road was leased as a fish and chip business, but it is now two houses. Frank retired in 1958 as Milton Road was sold, it continued to fry fish and chips for a while, but it is now a Chinese Take-Away.

Harold continued to sell fresh fish only in Tangier Road until he retired in 1960, the shop was sold and became a betting shop, it has since been turned into a house. When Harold retired the company was wound up." H.Barnett

25	George Fleet, Boot Maker
27	James Herbert, Clothier
29	Thomas Hall, Cycle Dealer
31	L Rabbetts, Optician

"He was the brother of the jeweller"

35 to 47 was Lucknow Terrace

33-37	Portsmouth Trade Union Club & Institute Ltd., here since 1923
43	Transport & General Workers' Union, Divisional Office
45	Frederick Taylor, Accumulator Service
47	Payne Brothers, Ironmongers
49	Henry Potts, Hairdresser

51	William Walker, Wool Stores, in 1928 William Walker was here but selling beef and ham.
55	The Froddington, Landlord John Smith

First listed in the trade directories as the Plough & Spade in 1830. It was known as the Swiss Gardens from 1879 to 1898 becoming the Froddington Arms Hotel by 1910. It was a Biden's house by 1880.

here is Somers Road North another of the old lanes of the city. This was called originally Green Lane and included in its length what is now Somers Road, Green Road and Castle Road.

St. Mary's Mission Church

Built in 1880, it was enlarged in 1888. It suffered slight bomb damage in 1941 and 1944. It closed on the 31st of December 1961 and was demolished in 1964

61	The Red Company Club was attached to the mission church.

In 1898 it is listed as St. Mary's Mission Club.

Each Mission Church had its own groups and organisations. These were the Women's Fellowship, the long established Men's clubs and the various youth organisations.

Men's clubs had sports clubs for cricket and football teams, and club rooms. Some of the clubs retained the title 'Company'. This dated from the end of the nineteenth century and was suggested by Sir Arthur Conan Doyle's book The White Company.

St. Boniface Mission had the White Company, St. Barnabas Mission the Blue Company and St. Marys Mission the Red Company.

The Red Company club room had once been a shop next door to the Mission Church. The club room was open every evening, with a bible class on Mondays. The club had flourishing football and cricket teams, the latter having most of its fixtures with country village clubs. The club also had regular summer camps, parties, concerts and dances.

63	Samuel Cook, Fruiterer
65	George Russell, Hair Dresser
67	Sidney Primmer, Baby Carriage Manufacturer

here is Fratton Grove

69	Mrs Annie Short, Furniture Dealer
71-97	Portsea Island Mutual Co-Operative Society Ltd., Central Stores

Previously there were smaller shops here which the Co-Op gradually acquired.

Portsea Island Mutual Co-operative Society was registered on the 24th of March 1873. The first shop was opened shortly afterwards on the 9th of May 1873 in Charles Street. This proved inadequate and a move was made to Curtis Terrace. In 1878 a piece of land in Chesterfield Terrace, Besant Road was purchased and a new shop built. The first site in Fratton Road was purchased in 1883 with an 80 foot frontage and a large new shop opened in 1887 housing grocery, boots, crockery, hardware and carpets. In 1898 the shop was extended to include drapery, footwear, menswear and furnishing departments. Further expansion was made in 1907 with an extended furniture department, 1913 new bakery and 1917 a cafe. On the 20th of July 1934 disaster befell and the premises were burnt down.

"I remember going with my mother and watching the Co-op building on fire."

"All the children including me from Fratton School failed to return after lunch as we stopped to witness the holocaust but we were gradually rounded up by Mr McDade and Mr Roberts armed with their canes."

A brand new department store rose from the ashes and was opened on the 4th of September 1937 after being built by Co-op staff under the direction of architect H.G.Wilding, however, this did not last for very long as it was blitzed during the 10th of January 1941 raid on the city.

"I remember 'Divi Day' at the Co-op. Mum used to take me to the Fratton Road Co-op before the fire. She would draw the 'Divi' then we went up in the lift to the tea rooms where I had a fancy cake and mum a cup of tea."

"Dad worked very hard for £8 10s for a 45 hour week as a storeman. I can remember the big fuss in the mid 50s when some of his workmates were caught knocking off groceries. At least one of them was jailed for that. Mum did casual co-op catering work on weddings and other functions, as did most of my aunties. Co-op dances were regular and cheap entertainment. The 'Divi' was very useful."

| 99 | Mrs Frances Preston, Furniture Dealer |
| 101 | Percy Levers, Beer Retailer |

First listed in 1863 as the Artillery Arms, in 1926 it changed name to the Penhale Arms when it was rebuilt to the designs of local architect A.E.Cogswell. It closed in 1981 and the pub front was removed and the building has been used as a shop since. It was a Bransbury's house by 1880, later Jewells and then Brickwoods.

103	George Corbin, Boot Maker has since been swallowed up by the enlarged shop of Constads.
105	W Rabbetts & Son, Watch Repair
	One son became an optician the other stayed here as a jeweller. Became a branch of T.Constad & Son by 1971
107	Edward Cole, Pork Butcher
	Perhaps remembered by most as Leslie's, Antique dealers, buyers of antiques, jewellery, binoculars etc. who are listed here from 1956.
109	Dittman & Malpas Ltd., Corn Merchant
	"We bought biscuits for our dog and bran for the rabbit there"

here is Garnier Street

The Dog And Duck

| 115 | Dog & Duck, Landlord Mrs B Danagher |
| | There has been a public house here for many years. It is first mentioned in 1729. It was sold in 1750 to William Pike the brewer. It is named after the corner of the field in which it was built and was known as Dog & Duck Corner. It closed in 1981 and |

14

in 1984 the single storey bar extension added by Brickwoods was removed and the premise converted into a bank.

here are Freeland Cottages

So named because the area of land in front of the cottages, which is now the car park of the old cinema, was not known to be owned by anybody. The land has never been built on just in case the ownership is proved. There were four cottages.

The Troxy Super Cinema was built on the site of the cottages. It was opened by Tivoli (Portsmouth) Ltd on the 8th of December 1936. It sat 1417 on the ground floor and 512 in the balcony. Like the Rex it was used as a store during the war from the 11th of November 1941, re-opening as a cinema on the 10th of September 1946. It later became part of the Essoldo Group. It reopened as the Essoldo Bingo Hall by 1976. When the former night club in Arundel Street was closed and converted into a bingo hall the one here closed and the building was last in use as a cash and carry warehouse.

"The Troxy was the last world in style, a massive sloping structure. The electric organ would rise up in front of the screen rendering all the 1936 ditties."

129   The Guardsman, Landlord Leonard Hibbs

Again a public house of long standing although it started life as the Britannic Coffee House in 1759. It became the King & Queen public house by 1768 and kept this name until 1880 when it was renamed The Guardsman. It closed in 1976 and was converted into a restaurant.

131-133   Timothy Whites Ltd., Chemists

One of the well-known chain of local shops was here for many years. Timothy White came to Portsmouth in 1848 and founded his business that expanded to cover a large area of the country. When he first came and took over premises in Commercial Road at least one local resident, William Tarring was not too pleased as can be judged from notes he wrote on the 1850s "Nearly opposite was a chemist's shop. When the proprietor (whose name I have for the time forgotten) retired to become Borough Chamberlain, the business was taken over by the dear darling delightful TIMOTHY WHITE, who then commenced to lay the foundations of his cheap and nasty business by selling pills at one counter and putty at another."

"They sold everything in the ironmongery line. They were there for years after the war."

here is Arundel Street named after the Portsmouth to Arundel Canal that ended at the Commercial Road end of the street.

135   Harry Denham, Beer Retailer
From 1865 to 1880 the Fratton Brewery.
Listed from 1898 to 1958 as a beer retailer.

139   William Billing, Butcher
"One of Mum's butchers was Billings almost opposite Clive Road and if Mum sent me, Mr Billings would sing 'You can't get many pimples on a pound of pickled pork!' Billings later moved to Meadow Street."

141   Peter Arnett, Fishmonger

143   Fleming, Reid & Co. Ltd., Scotch Wool Stores

145   Selway & Sons, Outfitters

147-151 Southern Trojan Services Ltd., Motor Agents

here is Coish Lane named after the local family.

155   Coish & Sons, Builders

157-159 Portsea Island Mutual Co-Operative Society Ltd., Butchers
By 1938 it had become the Co-Operative Funeral Furnishers.

161   Alfred Williams, Boot Dealer

163   Edward Crispin, Grocer

165   Arthur Reynolds, Dress Agency

167   Edward Lewis, Chemist

169   Harry Evans & Son, Clothier

171-173 S. Ramsdale, Draper

175-177 Ernest Vincent, Beer Retailer
From 1863 to 1910 was listed as the Trafalgar Brewery. It is next listed in 1956 as the Old Trafalgar which it renamed until 1981 when it was closed and converted into flats. It was a Trigg's House then King's and by 1891 Palmers.

here is Stamford Street

179   Frank Payne, Wine & Spirit Merchant

181   Henry Martin, Tobacconist

183   Jacks, Confectioners

185   Arthur Benney, Hair Dresser he was also at number 10

189   Walter Cutler, Tobacconist

191   Mrs Ellen Guggisberg, Confectioner was still a confectioner in 1940, taken over by Walter Cutler by 1946 who by 1956 was only at 191 as a Wool Specialist.

193   J.H.Lloyd & Co., Printers

195   Chapman's Laundry, Receiving Office

197   William Adams, Dentist

here is Fitzroy Street

201	Ivan Veck, Musical Instrument Dealer
203	H.R. Taylor & Co. Ltd., Manufacturing Stationers
203A	George Payne, Boot Manufacturer
205	Saville Hanbury, Physician & Surgeon

Globe Electric Theatre, Pannell Bros. Proprietor.

> The licence was granted on 29th of April 1913 to Mr Pannell. It sat 543. Closed by the 10th November 1936 for modernisation, it reopened on the 18th of May 1937 by which time it had been renamed The Rex and was owned by Tivoli (Portsmouth) Ltd seating 400 on the ground floor with 90 in the balcony. It was used as a store from 9th of December 1941 until the 10th July 1945. In later years it operated as an 'adult' cinema, The Tatler, before becoming a Classic for a short time. It is now a snooker club. "The 'Bug-Hutch'. One could get scared by Sweeney Todd or Boris Karloff and be flea bitten for the princely price of 2d."

Carnegie Free Library, Branch of City of Portsmouth Public Libraries.

> Built in 1905 to the designs of local architect A.E.Cogswell.

213   Harry Western, Tailor

> This was known as Tokio Villa and next door was Albert Villa.

then there was a terrace of 13 houses to Church Road known as Clydesdale Terrace.

6   Edmund Hinks, Dentist

Clydesdale Terrace c1910

13   Hampshire & Isle of Wight Band of Hope Union

here is Church Road named since it was the last portion of the lane to the church from Portsea.

The Vicarage, this was occupied by the various curates of St. Mary's Church.

Senior Curate - Rev Henry Crick, Assistant Curates - Rev Archibald Franklin, Rev D Hoare, Rev Cyril Smith, Rev K Riches, Rev Sidney Clark, Rev Robert Stewart, Rev Oswald Batty, Rev Basil Westcott.

Portsmouth Parish Institute

St. Mary's Sunday School

> "The Parish Institute housed the Sunday School and the Northern Secondary School for Boys."

249   Museum Gardens, Landlord John Wiseman

> This public house has had several changes of name even in the past. From 1830 to 1863 it was the Shipwrights Arms, by 1865 the Shipwrights Arms And Museum Tea Gardens. From 1875 to 1986 just Museum Gardens.
>
> It was re-fronted in 1899, architect A.E.Cogswell who was also responsible for another new front in 1932. On 10 May 1986 it reopened as the Frog And Frigate. In 1989 yet another change of name this time to the Landmark

The shops and houses from here to 325 on the corner with Lake Road were demolished when Lake Road was realigned and the new flats built.

251   Fire Brigade Station

253   Police Station & Quarters

These two premises were built on the site of a former Tramway Stable that dated back to the days of horse drawn trams.

"Fratton Police Station was built in 1907. In the early days of Policing the Police & Fire Brigade were virtually as one. Hence the Police & Fire embellishments on the facade. The building was quite large with an extension at the back. Originally it was known as Central Bridewell, after the London Prison. It served as a local police barracks with live in accommodation for about 15-20 men. There were 8 or 9 rooms available for this and the older members of the force had a room to themselves whilst the younger ones shared at about 2-3 to a room. Owing to shift work with your room mates coming and going you did not get a lot of rest. There was no space for wardrobes but everyone had a locker in the passage for his 'civvies'. Quite often you came off duty only to find your clothes had been borrowed by your mate knowing that you would not want them whilst on duty. There were never any hard feelings though.

There was a communal kitchen. The cook was a Mrs Grace who only cooked dinners so, depending on your shift you had her dinner (warmed up if necessary) for breakfast, lunch, tea or supper. P.C.s took it in turn on a monthly basis to do the catering. All the vegetables came from Bennetts the greengrocers just along the road. They sometimes got it on tick and paid up at the end of the month. With pay at £3 per week it was always a bit of a struggle. One of the perks when catering was that you made sure you had any spare food. Personal food lockers were available but with ever hungry constables about any food left in them did not have a very high survival rate. We remember a roast chicken left in there when one of the lads went on duty only to have turned mysteriously into a bare boned carcass by the time he came off! Cakes left there also tended to shrink. The bread was also rock solid so instead of being eaten it was often soaked in water and used for bread fights. The (unfortunate?) duty officer had the job of cleaning up after meals.

To the right of the building as you faced it was the Police House. The duty officer was on for eight hours at a time. His wife acted as matron and served food to any prisoners. The quarters at the rear were known as the Section House and had their own matron. One we remember well was Mrs Sugars, known to all as 'Lil'.

We joined in 1936 at 18 years old as apprentice firemen at £2 per week. There were ten of us all told and all trained as firemen. We were proficient

Fratton Fire & Police Station

19

in all aspects of firefighting including manning the pumps although this job was usually the prerogative of the driver. Every scrap of brass had to be polished and we had plenty of fire drills. Virtually all the big fires were handled by the police. The fire engine was an old Ford with a 45ft Ajax extending ladder. It was equipped sparsely with a standpipe and a key, a few rolls of hose and one or two extinguishers. If you were off duty at the time of a fire alarm you leapt on board just to get some overtime. However, this was paid in time, hours off, not money.

As you face the building on its left were a set of concertina doors, this was the garage area for the fire engine. In the middle was what was called the alley. This was the main entrance and had no door as such, an iron grill could be placed across but seldom was. Immediately to the right was the inspector's office and behind this the duty office. The building had about six cells for male offenders and a smaller number for females. A jailer was provided. The upper floors housed C.I.D. and the entrance to this domain was around the back and up an old iron staircase. You then crossed a balcony known as the 'Iron Bridge'. This was a very useful place for getting your own back on anyone who made himself unpopular simply by pouring a bucket of water over him as he passed underneath and disappearing poste haste!

We had our own billiard table with a split baize and an incomplete set of balls. I, Gron, was there 'til about the end of 1940. At this time the fire engine bay was turned over to the Civil Defence. Living in was abolished but meals were still available. The building was still kept in use as a Police Station but the section house was not used as such again. The station stayed in use until the amalgamation of the Portsmouth & Hampshire Forces at which time it became redundant and it was eventually demolished in the 1960s"

Ken Hampton & Gron Evans   PCs retd.

255 to 267 was Museum Terrace
- 257   Dockyard Impartial Coal Society Ltd.
- 259   Buckingham Bros. Ltd., Monumental Masons
- 263-265   Head & Co. Ltd., Milliners

269 to 281 was St. Angus Terrace
- 269   Buckland Branch Post Office
- 273   Mrs F Dipnall, Pastrycook
- 275   Mrs W Hayward, Florist moved to 263 by 1938 and was later run by Barrells
           "The son of the florist became a famous choreographer."
- 277   Charles Howard, Hairdresser
- 279   John Bennett, Tobacconist
- 281   Mrs K Fitzgerald, Leather Seller

here is Gunner Street named after William Gunner of Gunner & Renny solicitors who dealt with the sale of land in the area

283	William Trim, Cycle Repairer
285	Brunswick Family Laundry Co. Ltd., Receiving Office
287	George Robinson, Beer Retailer
	Listed as Off licence or wine merchants from 1898 to 1967

289 to 301 was Garibaldi Terrace

291	Coysh & Smith, Plumbers
293	Miss Mabel Griffiths, Art Needlework Depot
295	A Smith & Sons, Shop Blind Makers
297	Bert Lawrence, Hair Dresser
299	Arthur Dikes, Fried Fish Shop the business was in the family from 1923 to 1967.
301	Mrs Rose Newnham, Beer Retailer
	First listed in the trade directories as a beer retailer in 1874 and last shown in 1967. In the 1887 directory it is shown as The Solent. It was a Browning's brewery house.

here is Kilmiston Street named after the village where the Ridge family who were local landowners lived.

305 to 317 was St. Clair Terrace

305	Bertram Winter, Wireless Dealer
307	Stanton's Restaurant
309	Arthur Hoad, Florist
311	Alex Matthews, Draper
313	Charles Gray, Boot Repairer
315	Sidney Snellgrove, Boot Stores
317	Edward Bray, Fruiterer
319	Thomas Guy, Tailor
321	Charles Clark, Newsagent
323	Henry Stebbens, Confectioner
325A	Southern Estates Office, Business Transfer Agents
325A	Southern Enquiry Agents, Enquiry Agents
325	John McIntosh, Chemist later Boots The Chemist

Returning to Fratton Bridge and on the east side

Lloyds Bank Buildings

	Alfred Cartwright, Accountant
	Central Association of Accountants Ltd. (Southern Counties District)
2A	Tremlett, Chemist
2B	Valentino Fontana, Confectioner the premises were absorbed into Tremletts by 1962.

"It all started in the late twenties with my parents coming to Portsmouth to join other members of my father's family who were already established in cafes and restaurants in the City. Both parents came from the same village in the Alps of North West Italy near the City of Ivrea. Mother, Romilda Fontana, nee Piantino, came to England in 1908 at the age of 11 to join her uncle and enter service in London. My father Valentino Silvio Fontana, came over when he was fifteen years old to join his three sisters and brother who were already working in the hotel trade in London. My father served an apprenticeship as a confectioner at the Royal Automobile Club but because of the shortage of sugar in the First World War, he was also trained in general cookery. Over the subsequent years he gained good quality catering experience in London; including a spell at Harrods, and winning a gold medal in 1928 at Olympia.

Like many immigrants of peasant background my parents' ambition was to own their own business and when 2B Fratton Road came on the market they decided that it could hold good prospects. The then owner, Mr James Cox, had it as a sweet shop where amongst the others he sold his own products. My father, being a master confectioner took the business over in 1930 as a going concern but the slump made it difficult to make ends meet. So it was decided to reduce the sweet making and open the workshop at the back as a restaurant, with a small kitchen at the side. The rest of the premises carried on as before, a sweet shop in the front, with two tables where one could have just a cup of tea or coffee or cold drink; such as still lemonade made from a bright yellow sugary powder mixed with water and cooled by ice in a glass barrel. Upstairs were our living quarters consisting of two small rooms and a butler sink on the landing, no bathroom but an outside loo at the side downstairs.

In the cafe my parents started by serving what was at the time somewhat up-market fare such as roast chicken. This proved popular with a few retired officers in the area, but not with the majority who were unaccustomed to it and simply could not afford it. My mother, being more business minded, solved the problem by insisting they lowered their sights and catered for what she described as the 'Fish & Chips, Bread & Butter, Cup of Tea Brigade'. This proved to be a very successful strategy. There were many regulars for lunch from the local business community; such as Mr Blake of Bowler & Blake the estate agents in Goldsmith Avenue, Mr Walker of Walker's dairy who always swamped his food in salt, staff from Dring's and Palmer's factories nearby, and the manager and staff from Lloyd's Bank on the corner. When I see Dad's Army, I always think of the latter group. The summer season was our boom time. Southsea was popular with visitors and in August the City was full. Householders all round the Fratton area let out rooms for a few shillings a week. It was not unknown for families to let off all their rooms for bed and breakfast whilst they themselves slept in a shed or tent in the garden. All these extra mouths needed feeding and because of our good reputation many came all the way back from the sea front to have lunch at the 'Bridge'. Bed and Breakfast visitors were not allowed back into their lodgings till 6pm so they had to eat out. We were crowded out from July to September between 12 noon and 2pm. We served a three-course lunch consisting of soup (mostly the packeted variety), Roast & Two Veg followed by a pudding all for the princely sum of 1/- (5p); or 1/3d (5.25p) if you had bread and butter and a cup of tea as well. Mother always said that the extra 3d was where the profit was. Quite a lot came back in the evening for supper eating Fish & Chips, Ham, Egg and Chips etc., plus the bread and tea of course. Our other welcome source of trade was when Pompey were playing at home. Before the match we did a roaring trade in cigarettes and sweets, when we often needed three people serving behind the counter to cope. After the match many would come in for tea, we often had supporters for both clubs in at the same time, but there was never any trouble. The cafe was open till 10pm, but we were not allowed to serve anything from the shop after 8pm. I can remember three of our waitress' names, Elsie, Joyce and Pat. As my mother was a trained parlourmaid, and had been a J.Lyons Nippy, she made sure they were trained to do a good job in the Cafe. These girls, who often came to us straight from school at 14, were expected to do the cleaning and serving in the shop as well. There was also a Kitchen maid to peel potatoes and wash up.

The kitchen was a bit primitive by todays standards. In general my parents bought the food for the cafe fresh every morning. We had no fridges, only an icebox to keep food fresh in. The ice was delivered twice weekly from the ice factory in Sackville Street. It came in blocks about 1 foot by 1 foot by 3 foot and was placed in the top of the ice box and as it melted the water drained out at the back. In warmer weather the ice had to be replaced more frequently and so had to be collected by ourselves. My old pushchair was used for this.

Once the Cafe was established, the only sweets that my dad continued to make was Almond Brittle and Easter Eggs. The eggs were freshly made in the run up to Easter using a large collection of moulds he had. Large blocks of Cadbury's chocolate were bought and melted down in a water bath to the right temperature, which my father could judge just by touch. Get the temperature wrong and the eggs came out looking mouldy rather than shiny brown. My father made marzipan flowers and used them to decorate the larger eggs; he had a great artistic skill at this. The undecorated eggs were wrapped in brightly coloured tinfoil. From about February till Easter this took up most of his spare time, leaving mother to run the shop. As a youngster I often helped him, sometimes by tasting the broken eggs! Invariably we had sold the lot by Easter Saturday evening.

Another busy time in the shop was just before Christmas when the shop would be brightly decorated and full of colourful boxes of chocolates and cotton wool (imitation snow) covered models filled with sweets and gifts for children.

All the woodwork in the shop was mahogany, there were mirrors all round and the counters were topped with marble. Every month the front window was cleaned out for redressing with my parents deciding what the layout was to be. Very often a window dresser from one of the sweet companies came and set up the centrepiece. As soon as the sun came round to shine in the window, generally about noon, a half blind was put up to protect the display, most of which were real sweets. Sweets that had been put in the window for a while could not be sold ordinarily, they were put on bags with odd scraps of other sweets to be sold as penny 'dusties' to children. Good value, but slightly peculiar taste. I did not bother with these I used to sneak round the back and help myself. One old customer recently recalled seeing me, as a six-year-old, with my mouth crammed full, being told off by mother. We sold a whole range of sweets from the more expensive continental things to cheaper locally made boiled sweets. Hostlers was the local sweet maker, their sweet factory was off Commercial Road where they made unwrapped boiled sweets at 3d per quarter pound and the famous Southsea Rock. The better boiled sweets by Pascall's were about 6d per quarter. A popular line at the time were cashews, small scented coloured sweets sold by the ounce and used by young men as breath fresheners when going out on a date. Commercial travellers from various sweet firms often came in to take orders from my parents. My favourite traveller was Mr Yates who represented Pascalls. He was popular with me as he often gave samples.

The war brought many restrictions. Those Italians who were not naturalised were either interned, mostly on the Isle Of Man, or were asked to move at least 30 miles away from the coast, as one of my relatives had to do. My parents and most of my family were naturalised, so we stayed.

The black-out, raids and rationing caused many changes. After dark one had to enter the shop via a 'light lock' to prevent light showing out. This consisted of a hardboard and timber structure round the door with a heavy curtain through which one entered the shop after closing the front door behind you. The display window was empty except for a few pictures and, after the glass was blown out during the March raid, it was boarded up except for a small 2ft by 3ft window in the middle. Everything around looked dingy and neglected.

For every sweet we sold we had to cut coupons out of a person's ration book. The value of the coupons varied from month to month according to the ratio allowed. At the end of each month all coupons collected had to be counted and taken to the Ministry Food offices, then housed in what is now Mayfield School at North End. We were then allowed to replace the stocks we had sold. The trade in the cafe remained good because many people ate out in order to supplement their rations. However, we were not allowed to serve any meal that cost more than 5/- value. This measure ensured that no one ate too much and that the price was kept down. We had to note every meal served and send in a form recording this every month. From this the Ministry people calculated how much food we were allowed for the cafe for the next month. Occasionally some smartly dressed gent would come in and offer us a box of lard or case of eggs, no questions asked.

By the beginning of 1941 we had already experienced quite a lot of bombing, there was a surface shelter just around the corner in Selbourne Terrace and another one under the London and Manchester Insurance Offices just over the bridge. We sometimes used them, but more often than not we just went down into our own cellar; where by this time we had the cafe's kitchen. On the night of Friday the 10th January 1941 there was a severe bombing raid and the Fratton Hotel, opposite us, was burnt to the ground. Dick Tremlett the pharmacist, out next door neighbour, was our local Air Raid Warden, and I remember him coming in and getting us to move to the shelter round the corner because he feared that the shell of the hotel would collapse on top of us. That night was one of the most frightening I ever experienced. I was only 12 and did not like the idea of dying so soon. After that we just took raids in our stride, and there were many more of them. The day after the big raid we, with lots of other Portsmouth people, went to North End where we caught a bus out to Drayton and were fortunate to get lodgings with a very nice couple, Mr and Mrs Brown in Portsdown Avenue. In the morning we came down into town to run the

2A & 2B Fratton Road

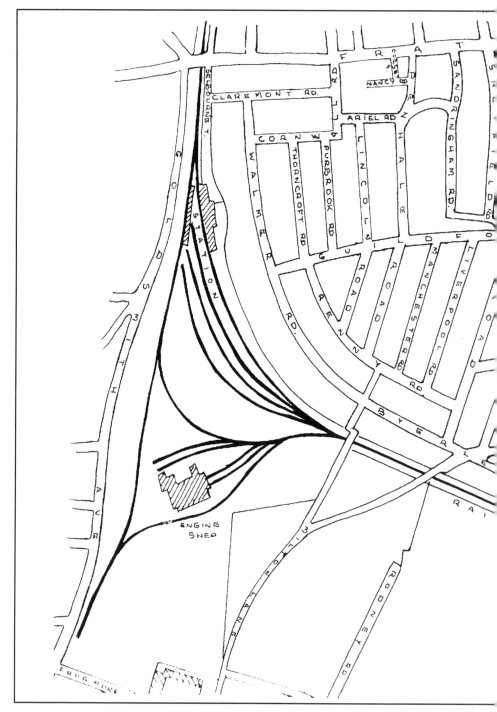

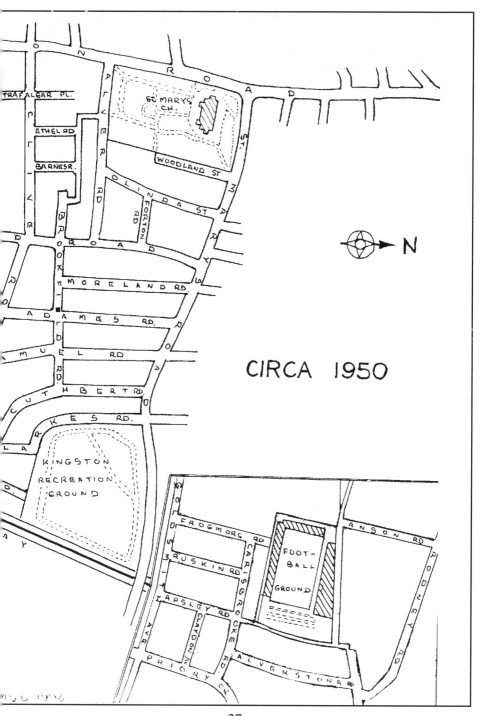

CIRCA 1950

business. In my case go to school, and in the evenings returned to Drayton to avoid the bombing. Whilst there my father joined the Cosham Home Guard Company, and whilst with them he ran the catering for their camps. Later he was called up and joined the then newly formed Army Catering Corps where he served till the war ended. In the meantime my mother and I then a fifteen year old ran the business. Postwar saw the business still running successfully. But we no longer lived over the shop as my parents had bought a house in North End by that time.

We were still popular with the Football crowd. These were the years of the First Division Championship when the crowds were very great. However, holiday makers became less plentiful. My parents managed to carry on till the late 50s when partly due to ill health they decided to close the cafe. The final closed sign went up on the remaining sweet shop in 1962 when Tremlett took over the premises to move his pharmacy from 2A to 2B, because the Bank wanted to expand into 2A."   Velmo (Val) Fontana

2	Walter Meade, Tobacconist
8	The City Service, Dyers & Cleaners
10	Arthur Benney, Hairdresser

"My own feelings about Mr Benney, the ladies hairdresser, are somewhat mixed. He certainly gave us a lot of business, as we (The Bridge Cafe) used to supply tea and coffee to his customers undergoing long-winded permanent waving treatment. It looked like electric torture. He was the first in the area to have a permanent waving machine. To my great disgust, as an eight-year-old, I was taken to him to have my hair permed (me a boy) to enable me to act as a page boy at a cousin's wedding. I had to wear light blue velvet trousers and a frilly blouse!"

12	Charles Stonham, Butcher
14-16	Mason & Bennett Ltd., Hosiers who were also in to London Road and Albert Road. The numbers changed to 16-18 during the time the shop was here.
18	British Standard Boot Repairs, Sidney Gandy
20	W & R Fletcher Ltd., Butchers
22	Lewis Barnfather, Ladies' Outfitter
24	Harry Slape, Fishmonger

"He was an interesting character always ready with a joke. He was alleged to be the local 'bookies' runner', illegally collecting bets off people and seeing to it that the bookie got them; the local police seemed to turn a blind eye to these goings on. Mum and Dad always had a bet on the Derby or the National, and somehow Harry always seemed to be involved."

26-28	Charles Welton, Government Contractor
30	Thomas Kilner, Chemist
32	Hayling Island Egg Producers Ltd.
34	George Cooper, Butcher
36	James Gwyer, Boot & Shoe Stores
38	Smith & Vosper Ltd., Bakers
40	Gordon Cole, Saddler

42-44 was Grosvenor Terrace

42	Miss Freda Pearce, Confectioner
44	Amalgamated Engineering Union (Div Office)
44	The "John Pile" Memorial Meeting Rooms, Proprietress Mrs Pile
46-48	R.L.Evelyn Ltd., Toy Dealer & Wholesale Stationers
	Was later Victor Value then Tescos.
50	Fratton Road Branch Post Office
52	Mrs Helen Riches, Ladies' Outfitter
54	John Palmer Ltd., Brush Manufacturers, Garage
	Founded in 1870 in Surrey Street making Victory Brushes. The firm went bankrupt in 1995.
	Now Excelsior Coaches garage.
56	John Allen Ladies' Outfitter

58 to 68 were Magdala Terrace

58	Watson & Harnwell, Florist
60	Wild Bros., Wireless Dealers (1934 to 1948), Wild Bros., Model Dealers (1951 to 1953), Wild Bros., Electrical Supplies, radio engineers, model railway accessories. (1956 to 1962), Wild Bros., Electrical Accessories (1964 to 1966)

"Back in the 50s shops of interest for young boys were few and far between. To be dragged down to the town was a punishment. Yes, the sweet and toy shops had some sort of interest but a shop that a twelve year old would go out of his way to look at was very rare indeed, yet Fratton Road had not one but two such establishments. Just before Fratton Bridge on the eastern side was Wilde Bros. This shop had been going since well before the war and my father had been a regular customer in his premarital days. What did it sell? Model trains! Not just your ordinary Hornby stuff - very good but Oh! the rails. In Wilde Bros the rails looked like rails and the engines - what variety. At this time (around 1952) Hornby had about four or five different engines, Triang were just coming onto the scene, Trix were established but left a bit to be desired, but at Wildes we had Graham-Farish and (I think) Bassett-Lowke were still available. Different scales

but the quality and finish were superb. They did however, have one setback the price! From memory this started about 50% higher than Hornby and increased the further up-market you went. This obviously led to more window-gazing than buying. I suppose at that period, those who could afford such desirable and expensive 'toys' were few and far between and although the shop sold other electrical equipment it eventually closed down. The other Mecca was further up the road almost opposite what was the Rex Cinema, Robin Thwaites (see number 248)"
Malcolm Garlick

62	Singer Sewing Machine Co. Ltd.

"I often got into trouble as one of their repairers. We were supposed to suggest to the customer that a new machine was required, but I would repair the old machine! Eventually I gave up the job."

64	S Pearce, Greengrocer
66-70	The Magpie, Landlord William Hammond

First listed in 1874 as a beer retailer it is named the Brickmakers Arms in 1887. It was rebuilt in 1894 to the designs of A.H.Bone the local architect or in 1901 by A.E.Guy depending which book you believe. At this time it was renamed the Magpie. It was a Browning's brewery house.

here is Cornwall Road

72	Charles Welton, Government Contractor

Victory Hall, Proprietors John Palmer Ltd
Proprietors Portsea Island Co-operative Society Ltd

84	Frederick Osborn, Undertaker
86-88	C.J.Hobbs & Co., Electrical Engineers
88	National Amalgamated Union of Shop Assistants (District Office)
90-92	Sanders Bros. (Stores) Ltd., Grocers
94-96	Lipton Ltd., Provision Merchants
98	Maypole Dairy Co. Ltd.

"I was 14 on the 28th April 1928 and my father died on the 29th. My mother was left with four children. Through some friends of my mother I finished up working in the Maypole. They were principally butter but did cheese and groceries as well. The shop was in Fratton Road, near where the Co-op Supermarket now stands. There were three shops there - the Maypole, Liptons and the Home & Colonial, all in competition. There was no set time of closing although most shops closed around 6 o'clock and on Friday and Saturday it was usually somewhere about 8 o'clock.

What the manager did was to send one or the other boys out to have a look at the other two shops. If they looked as if they were going to stay open we stayed open. No matter what time you closed - whether it be 8 or 9 - after that you did a stock take, and I know that I've walked along Fratton Road going home at midnight or twelve-thirty many a time.

Another of our jobs: they used to load us up with a basket of ready-made-up packs of margarine and butter. We had to go round with these things in a basket and try to sell them from door to door. At Christmas they used to do biscuits done up in tins and packages and they told us we had to go home and sell as many as we could to our friends and family and so on. It was part of our working hours and you never got any commission or anything like that. If you didn't sell many you got a blast; if you sold a lot someone would pat you on the head and that was it. I was paid ten shillings a week and there was no reduction because you worked for them - if you bought a pound of butter they didn't knock 2d off. I stuck that job until the March or April 1929."

Ron

100	Herbert Riches, Tobacconist
102	Home & Colonial Stores Ltd
104	World's Storcs Ltd.
106-114	Portsea Island Mutual Co-Operative Society Ltd., Drapers

110 was opened in 1930 as a drapery and fashion store joined in 1933 by a modern grocery store.

here is Nancy Road Later the road split in two and the part leading from Fratton Road was named Dorset Street. The Co-operative shops have since been built across the road.

116	Portsea Island Mutual Co-Operative Society Ltd., Grocers
118	George Peters & Co Ltd., Wine & Spirit Merchants

here is Penhale Road

128   Methodist Central Hall, Portsmouth Methodist Garrison & Naval Port Mission

The site was purchased in 1886 for £1,200. The first church was opened in 1889 on the 21st of March and was a corrugated iron chapel at the rear of the site that cost £510 4s 7d. In 1900 a new permanent building was opened on the 4th of July fronting onto Fratton Road at a cost of £4,675. The architects were Messrs Green & Brocklehurst of Liverpool. This building survived until 1927 when Fratton Road was widened and the church site reduced by 20 feet. The new Central Hall opened in 1928 on the 28th of October at a cost of £48,000. This building lasted until

1990 when it was demolished and replaced with a smaller church, halls and flats. The foundation stone was laid by Viscount Tonypandy on the 6th of December 1991. The new building was opened on the 10th of October 1992 by the then president of the Methodist Conference Rev Kathleen Richardson.

"Every Sunday evening my brother and I were taken by our Mum to hear the Reverend Lee preach hellfire and damnation to me, a sinner. At least he always seemed to be looking my way!"

130A   J Hocking, Wireless Engineer

130   J.B.Ward & Sons, Bakers

"I worked in Ward's cake shop it was situated underneath Wesley Central Hall. There were four shops, a florist, a confectioners and a hairdressers as well as Wards. All these shops were very old fashioned with high windows, dark paintwork and old sign writing above the premises. The shops had basements which were next to the crypt of the church.

Ward's was a very busy shop it was fortunate to have a bus stop right outside, needless to say myself (the manageress) and two assistants were very happy there. Fratton Road at that time, about 1948, was a very busy area. The main Coop brought a lot of trade to all shops, as at that time they paid out a dividend twice a year, so people could indulge themselves with things they could not normally afford, namely Wards cakes. Although it was post war, cakes were not plentiful. When we had our next days order phoned through, one of the assistants would paint on the window with white wash what would be available the next day, this would make sure we had a queue before we arrived to open the shop. This was the time of the first sliced bread which was wrapped in white waxed paper, not plastic as today. A large loaf cost 4½d to 5d, sliced, and 2¾d for a small one, rolls would cost 2 for a 1½d if available which wasn't often. Bread and cakes were wrapped in paper bags, carriers and cake boxes did not exist.

At that time if someone requested a wedding cake the bases were made of a mixture of very little fruit but darkened with burnt sugar, sometimes it came with marzipan, but icing sugar was very scarce so the cake was covered with a dummy cardboard decoration.

As time went on Mr Wilfred Ward (Company Director) retired and sold the business to A & E Hicks Ltd, bakers of Apsley Road, known as the Fratton Park Bakery. This was a very old established firm, they had bread rounds delivered by horse and cart. It was then taken over by De Havelands who were

Canadians renaming the shops Westons. All the shops were updated and they acquired two more making a total of twelve. When the shop was improved it looked odd against the other old fashioned shops.

As years went by and merchandise became plentiful, at Christmas and Easter we were able to display the goods more attractively. As I loved window dressing I used to go in Sundays to decorate the windows, after getting people to make sleighs and igloos etc. As now when you were busy till rolls always ran out, but in those days they were easier to replace than the computerised ones of today."

Pat Goldring

132   Miss Florence Hair, Confectioner

138 to 144 was Clanville Terrace

140-144   George Parnell & Co., Hosiers

KNOCKABOUT SUITS
FOR EVENING
and ...
HOLIDAY WEAR
IN NEAT AND DURABLE TWEEDS
21/- & 25/-

GEO. PARNELL.,
138-140, FRATTON ROAD

146   White & Lowery, Complete House Furnishers

here is Sandringham Road

152-156 W.Pink & Sons Ltd, Grocers

158   Old Red House, Landlord George Lean

First listed in the trade directories as the Red House in 1823 it had become the Old Red House by 1863. Rebuilt in 1959 as the Unicorn. It was a Pike Spicer's house.

here is Sheffield Road

164-168 Harold Seager, Wallpaper Merchants

They moved to Kingston Road following the loss of the premises in the war before returning to a new shop. By 1976 was H.Seager subsidiary of C Brewer & Sons Ltd.

170-172 Campions (Bakers) Ltd.

174   George Shipp, fruiterer

176   Herbert King, Newsagent

178   Henry Playfair Ltd., Boot & Shoe Stores

180   Miss Dorothy Cooper, Milliner

182   Portsmouth Voluntary Association for the Blind

here is Newcome Road

190-192   Mrs Edith Pounds, Beer Retailer
First listed as a beer retailer in 1874 by 1887 it is listed as The Old House At Home. It was rebuilt in 1924 to the designs of local architect A.E.Cogswell. Since 1954 it has been listed in the directories as The Electric Arms. It probably took this name when the new electric trams came to the town. It was a Young's brewery house.

194-196   Co-Operative Permanent Building Society

194-196   Morris Onion, House, Land and Estate Agent

194-196   Co-Operative Insurance Society Ltd.

198   George Wallen, Fried Fish Shop

200   Oakley's (Mrs Hawkley), Cycle Dealer

202-204   Thomas Stride, Builder

206-208   S Ramsdale, Draper

210   S & C Newton, Greengrocers

212   Martin Menist, Grocer there was a restaurant above.

here is Clive Road named after Lord Clive

216 to 252 was Trafalgar Place

216   Edward Harper, Tobacconist

218   Harold Harries, Draper

220   J Littlefield & Co, Inside & Outside Blind Makers

222   Albert Castle, Tailor

224   People's Prescription Service, Drug Stores

226   Ancient Order of Foresters

226-230   Foresters' Hall

230   Harry Rouse, Fruiterer

232   A Kingswell, Butcher

234   J.H.Lloyd & Co, Printers. They were here in the 1898 as stationers.

236   Eagle Sign Co., Sign Writers

238   Anderton Bros., Cycle Agents

240   The Frodden Billiard & Social Club

242   Salmons Tea Gift Shop

244   Portsmouth Savings Bank

248   Finlay & Co. Ltd., Tobacconists
Later became Robin Thwaites, Handicrafts & Mode! Makers "This specialised in model aircraft kits. They came in two types flying or solid. The flying were mainly Keil-Kraft, Vernon and Frog whilst the solids were dominated by Vernon in their yellow, black and red boxes. The flying models were much as they are

today, built of stringers, bulkheads and spars, much as the real thing. The solid kits were just roughly sawn lumps of balsa wood which had to be carved and sanded to shape, glued together with balsa cement, doped to colour and transfers applied. This was a time consuming, messy and sometimes dangerous job. Messy because of all the filing and sanding involved plus balsa cement (glue) could get everywhere. It formed a colourless skin on your fingers and we would often impress the girls by peeling it off and letting them think we were skinning ourselves. If it got on your clothes or the furniture it was impossible to get it off. Seeing as this was all done indoors, usually in the kitchen, you had to be careful. Dangers could arise in two ways. If you could afford them, you bought X-Acto modelling knives but if not, one of Dad's razor blades would do. Blood stained balsa was quite common! The other hazard was the dope used for colouring. It was highly inflammable and gave off similar fumes to the glues used by glue sniffers today. We were always breathing it in and sometimes it made us sick but we never got addicted to it. The advent of plastic kits within the next few years did away with these pleasures. The models in the shop window were always much better than ours and although the shop staff were always ready with advice and would always sell you something that would do the job. It was not until many years later that what we should have bought was a large bucket of patience! These shops were such an attraction that we would even spend valuable pocket money on the bus fare from Cosham, spend everything we had and have to walk home!" Malcolm Garlick

252   Harold Groves, Tool Merchant – still a tool merchants today

254   Trafalgar Arms, Landlord Harry Cowdrey

First listed in the trade directories as the Trafalgar Tavern in 1863, from 1898 it has been known as the Trafalgar Arms. It was rebuilt in 1926 to the designs of local architect A.E.Cogswell. It was a Jewell's brewery house by 1880.

Between the public house and the next shop is an alley on the shop side of this is a plaque with the wording

Trafalgar Place

1806

256   Charles Dunster, Hairdresser

258   Walter Cassidy, Confectioner

here is Alver Road

Portsea Parish Church (St. Mary's)

The original church of St. Marys was built in around 1166. It survived until 1843 when Thomas Owen the local architect produced plans for a larger church. This retained the tower from the old church and replaced the remaining nave and chancel with a large flint faced building. This too proved too small for the needs of the church and in 1883 the present church was built. This was designed by Sir Arthur Blomfield and largely paid for by W.H.Smith.

"At Kingston Churchyard towards Olinda Street were tombstones so placed that they resembled the trenches from World War 1. Many a battle was fought among the kids much to the dismay of old ladies taking their daily stroll."

here are St. Mary's Road and St. Mary's Crescent
The houses and shops from here to Manor Road were demolished when the St. Marys Road junction was improved and the school expanded.

270	M Filer & Son, Tailors
272	Frank Codlin, Confectioner
274-276	John Bryson, Florist

284 to 286 was Alpha Terrace

284	Henry Robinson, Cycle Manufacturer
286	Union Jack Char-A-Bancs (B.Shepherd) later the Imperial Saloon Coaches, Proprietor T.Bruce (1934 to 1946). The firm was acquired in 1947 by Hants And Sussex although in 1948 it is still listed as T.Bruce. 1951 to 1953 Hants & Sussex Motor Services Ltd.
286	Burnard & Sons, House Agents
288	Herbert Dore, Wallpaper Merchant, Paints, Varnishes etc. The business has been in the family from at least 1898.

here is Cardigan Road a road that has now disappeared due to expansion of the school.

290 to 300 was Manor Terrace

290	Charles Manship, Hair Dresser
294	Reginald Wolfe, Fishmonger
300	Harry Warren, Confectioner
302	Charles Whillier, Beer Retailer
	In 1887 is listed as Manor House but only as Beer Retailer from 1898 to 1953

here is Manor Road

304	Dye & Harrison, Grocers
306	Mrs Dorothy King, Confectioner
308	George Harris, Butcher (1923 to 1946)
	Doreen, Art Needlework, Mrs E.Harris (1948 to 1976)
310	In 1882 the premises are listed as a private house. The first commercial use was from 1886 to 1888 Joseph Bewsey,

Bootmaker. It was then listed as various watchmakers: 1890 to 1894 Walter White, Watchmaker; 1896 to 1898 William Fenn, Watchmaker; 1900 Thomas Burgess, Watchmaker & Jeweller; 1901 to 1902 Frank Edmonds, Jeweller & Engraver; 1904 to1918 Edgar Prance, Watchmaker; 1920 to 1921 Edward Weekes, The Modern Jeweller. The Constad family are first listed in 1923: 1923 to 1940 Thomas Constad, Watchmaker; 1946 to 1948 Tobias Constad, Watchmaker, 1951 to 1967 T Constad & Son; 1971 to 1976 T Constad & Son Ltd

The dates given in directories are often a few years out by the time information has been collected and printed also in this case the name is also wrong.

"The firm was started in 1920 by Tobias Constad, when he arrived from the continent and bought the shop from Edward Weekes. Tobias was apprenticed to a watchmaker at the age of twelve. In 1951 one of his sons, Mervyn who joined the business after the war, formed the limited company, T Constad & Son, that is still trading today. The shop retained its flat front until 1960 when the present shop front was fitted. Later the business expanded to include the former USA Studio at 312. When the shop was threatened with demolition another shop formerly Rabbetts near the main Co-op was purchased."

There are also branches at Waterlooville and another at Petersfield.

312   U.S.A. Studios, Photographers
"The premises were incorporated into Constad's shop when the proprietor retired."

314   Portsmouth Radical Club

314A   Arthur Sidebottom, Tobacconist

316   John Huntly, Fruiterer

318   Percy Hellyer, Confectioner
"On Sundays I bought three comics there; Rainbow, Bubbles and Chicks Own."
"On the vacant ground next to the Florist, that stretched back to Shakespear Road along the length of Hampshire Street, a fair came twice a year. They had the normal stalls with roundabouts and dodgem cars"
"Earlier there was a timber yard here"

324   Florist Inn, John Hutchings
First listed in 1874 as The Florist it took its name from nearby nurseries. It was rebuilt in 1924 to the designs of local architect A.E.Cogswell at a cost of £1,827. It was a Mansbridge's brewery house.

An 1838 map of the area shows the site which eventually became the corner of Beeston Street and Fratton Road to be a large garden with a cottage adjacent to a large plot of arable land both owned by Charles Emery. The garden plot and cottage were occupied by John Crockford. John Crockford, seedsman is mentioned in the 1852 directories. From 1863 to 1870 John Crockford Florist and Seedsman at 23 Buckland Road mentioned in the trade directories and rate returns. 314 Fratton Road is listed as John Crockford, florist in 1874 succeeded by Charles Crockford by 1886 as a nurseryman.

The present landlord, Robin Wyatt, started his working life in the Dockyard as an apprentice Fitter and Turner. His family has been in the licenced trade for over 100 years; first in The Solent and later at The Florist. The exterior was refurbished recently but a couple of the original leaded light windows can be seen in the lounge bar.

here is Beeston Street named after Beeston Field. This was a large field that used to lie to the east of Kingston Road and part of Fratton Road.

here is Hampshire Street

326 to 338 were Beaumont Terrace

326-328   C Cooke, Butcher

> "When Mr Cooke took over he renovated the shop and turned it into a butcher's shop. It opened with great gusto and at Christmas had a big Christmas show. It also had at the storehouse in Hampshire Street where a show of prize winning cattle from Smithfield Market. These were later slaughtered and sold as Christmas beef in the shop."   Charlie Hutchins
>
> later became Central Portsmouth Conservative Club

330   Edward Evans, Greengrocers

332   Mrs Margaret German, Grocer

334   Creed & Lawrence, Outfitters. By 1937 they had moved to Kingston Road.

334A   Harold Gutteridge, Ticket Writer

336   F Millward, Hairdresser

338 to 326 was Beaumont Terrace

338   The Express Dyers & Cleaners

340   John Best, Butcher

342   The Central Library, Proprietor Mrs A Burge later Dawn Libraries

346-348   John Freake, House Furnisher

350-352   Miss L Burch, Ladies' Outfitter

> "Further up Fratton Road was a milliners and baby wear shop, Burches' where I worked for a short time during the war. A Miss

Ferbrache was in charge and had been one of my Sunday School teachers."

354 Gilham Bros. Ltd., Fruiterers

356-362 John Barnes (Portsmouth) Ltd., Drapers

"As many of our older readers will no doubt remember, 10th January 1941 was the 'night of the blitz'. I remember it well as, like many others in the City, after a long days work, a quick bite for tea and I was back at my unpaid job in the Home Guard. We started at 1900 hours and with the full cooperation of Jerry we had an entertaining night.

Our area included the junction of Kingston Road, Fratton Road and Lake Road which was unfortunately due to receive a present from the Third Reich in the form that Portsmouth was to get to know only too well in the immediate future.

Opposite the top of Lake Road was a collection of buildings; Timothy Whites which occupied the first two shops in Kingston Road, Mortons the boot repairer, the Union Pub, Barnes the drapers and Gilhams fruit stores followed by a large gate that was the Fratton Road entrance to Avens food store in Beeston Street. This street ran parallel to Fratton Road along the backs of the previously mentioned premises.

When we arrived Barnes was on fire. As the corporal in charge I told my mate to see what he could do about saving Timothy Whites which we knew contained inflammable stuff, while I would do what I could to prevent the fire from reaching the food store (food was not the easiest thing to get at that time). Gilhams was also alight so the only thing to do was to douse before the fire spread to the food store. Our group was fortunate in that we had a small portable pump. This we connected to the hydrant in the pavement outside the Tramway Pub. With the aid of this we succeeded in our task. With no long term training in the art of fire fighting the logical thing to do seemed to us to get as much water into the flames as possible. We were fortunate in having the pump at our disposal and eventually after completely flooding the buildings which were on fire and also Mortons and Gilhams, which were not, we finally won!

It was a long, tiring job but eventually the lot was put out. The last thing alight was a severed gas pipe. This we covered with wet earth until it was smothered. By the time we had finished and got everything sorted out it was 0400 hours. This came out at nine hours without a break but in those days you did not stop to think how long it took, whose job it was or who was going to pay you, you just got on and did it."   Len Bufton

364	G & W Morton, Boot Makers
366	Frank Smith, Beer Retailer

366   From 1875 to 1887 was the Union Brewery. The premises are listed as a beer retailer in 1874 and named The Union in 1887. It was rebuilt in 1911 to the designs of architect J.J.Cotton. Closed by 1966

Guildford Road

East Side

45	Walter Johnson, Cooked Meat Vendor
87	Joseph Savage, Fried Fish Shop
93	Mrs C.Potts, Greengrocer
99	Robert Reynolds, Grocer
101	William Castle, Furniture Dealer
103	Walter Jeall, Butcher
105	Mrs Henrietta Oxford, Shopkeeper
107	George Snook, Builder (1934 to 1964) who was in 1923 an ironmonger, 1928 a decorator
109	Frank Holmes, Dairyman 1898; James Walker, Dairyman 1923 to 1951; Walkers Dairy 1953 to 1958; Gauntlett And Walkers Dairy 1960 to1982; Gauntletts 1983 to1987

The site is now housing

"Uncle Jack used to drive a milk lorry for Walkers in Guildford Road in the 50s. I went with him a couple of times, helping shift crates of milk during deliveries to cafes, restaurants and shops. Aunt Rene worked the steam sterilisation of milk churns, a very hard manual job, lifting the heavy steel churns in and out of the steam steriliser. I remember admiring this slightly built woman in rubber apron and boots doing this heavy lifting, with hot steam spraying over her in the open yard in all weathers."

119	The Connaught Arms, Alfred Shotter

1891 Built for Lush's Brewery it was named after Queen Victoria's son the Duke of Connaught who was Lieut Governor of Portsmouth. The name has changed slightly over the years from Connaught Hotel to the Connaught Arms and the Connaught Arms Hotel. It reopened on 3/9/1993 after a £50,000 refurbishment

121	Arthur Thomas, Decorator
139	William Fyfe, Police Court Missionary

West Side

14	George Bradfield, Plumber
22	Mrs Martha Kill, Beer Retailer

Listed from 1887 to 1976 as a beer retailer

24	Edward Kingswell, Shopkeeper
52	Edward Gear, Beer Retailer
	Listed from 1887 to 1948 as a beer retailer
54	Roberts & Parnell, Pawnbrokers
	"There was a pawnbroker's shop in Guildford Road, where my Mother lost some of her treasures."
54A	Arthur Derrick, Greengrocer
68	Edgar Trenear, Insurance Agent
70	Harry Hoar, Decorator
92-94	James Boyle, Garage.
	In 1923 this is listed as the Sheffield Sanitary Laundry proprietor James Boyle. In 1928 the garage is listed at both numbers with The Nelson Laundry at 92. It is now two houses.
102	Albert Pike, Boot Repairer
104	Charles Hide, Confectioner
106	Mrs Mary Hide, Greengrocer
108	Harry Randall, Drug Stores
110	Frank Dore, Hairdresser
112	Frank Jordan, General Dealer
114	George Copps, Cooked Meat Vendor
116	Joseph Edwards, Cycle Maker
118	Frederick Smart, Confectioner
124	Albert Stemp, Fried Fish Shop
128	John Taber, Shopkeeper
134	William Jury, Electrical Engineer
	In 1928 was Your Service Garage, William Jury
142A	John Young, Greengrocer
168	John Ellis, Tailor
170	Lawrence Sparkes, Grocer

Lincoln Road, In 1889 advertised as building land for sale
North Side

| | Council School |
| 83 | Frank Wallis, Upholsterer |

South Side

46	William Brunnen, Decorator
64	Albert Stagg, Boot Repairer
	Reginald Stagg

Liverpool Road, named after the town.
South Side

| 59 | Arthur Stewart, Shopkeeper |

Lower Brookfield Road
South Side

5A	The Craftsman Club
	Oliver Gibsorne, Upholsterer
	Frederick Handsford, Baker

There is a curious building (7A) in the road which belongs to L.Harris, Restorer of Antique Furniture and Upholsterer. He has been there thirty one years and cannot be relocated because he has an appointed Day Use made in 1948. The building was originally a stable, the upper doors still remain. It is used by several small business all in separate numbers overflowing into Rateys Lane. Print Direct have been there for three and a half years. At one time there was a boys' club there, a sausage maker named Harris, a jazz club and E.Wallace a baker. His ovens used to stick out into the gardens of Barnes Road until the present Mr Harris removed them.

Manchester Road, named after the town.
North Side

1	Leonard Harris, Dairy
	"I had many a ride on Len Harris's milk float along Guildford Road. The dairy was a house just inside Manchester Road, the house was bombed during the war."
13	Samuel Mason, Decorator

Moorland Road
East Side

7	Sidney Marshman, Tailor

Nancy Road named after the Portsmouth family, Nance. It was originally called Nance's Row.
North Side

17-19	Maurice Ablitt & Son, Blacksmiths
	"Just along Penhale Road before you got to the school was a blacksmith's and I often watched a horse being shod on my way to school"
	"Opposite the Co-op just inside Nancy Road was an old-fashioned blacksmith's smithy where a lot of their work was shoeing horses. Always a crowd of schoolboys watching"
49	Albert Starkins, Carrier

Newcome Road listed in 1887 some house still in building.
North Side

1	Miss Alice Hughes, Dressmaker

13	Edward Main, Taxi Hire
95	Robert Kay, Shopkeeper

"The newsagent on the corner of Newcome and Guildford Road, where I used to have to go and buy Daisy powder for Mum when she had her headaches. One day the shopkeeper would not let her have any as she was having too many. The shop is still there"

97	Geoffrey Bennett, Butcher
157	Victor Linnington, Shopkeeper
189	Newcome Arms Hotel, William George Shotter

Listed in 1891 as a beer retailer, named from 1898 to 1953 the Newcome Arms Hotel, and from 1956 to 1976 as the Newcome Arms. In 1902 additions were made architect A.E.Cogswell. It was a Pike's brewery house

South Side

10	Miss A Pointon, Apartments
22	United Ancient Order of Druids, William Luff District Secretary
58	Samuel Pervin, Inspector of Water Works
60	Mrs Margaret Rook, Tobacconist
64	Stephen Burgess, Hairdresser
100	Henry Hale, China & Glass Dealer
102	Mrs Edith Tuffnell, Shopkeeper
102	D.Worsley, Cabinet Maker
104	Herbert Hill, Decorator
212	George Loft, Shopkeeper

Olinda Street

West Street

22	Charles Ellis, Furniture Remover by 1937 was at 27
60	John Finch, Motor Car for hire

"He used to dance and appeared on Come Dancing."

East Side

29	Edward Flegg, Beer Retailer

Beer retailer from 1887 to 1938

57	Alfred Muggeridge, Boot Repairer
63	Mrs Elizabeth Phillips, Beer Retailer

Beer retailer from 1887 to 1938

The east side is now Monson and Knollys House flats

Penhale Road, In 1889 the building land was for sale, it was named after farm or field

South Side

2-4	Maurice Ablitt & Son, Coach Builders

18	George Harvey, Shopkeeper, the family have been here for many years in 1898 Thomas Harvey is listed.
26	Hedley Worrall, Tailor
30	Mrs Annie Gardner, Shopkeeper
	Council School

"Good friends, friendly school dinner ladies, but I got into trouble a bit with some of the teachers. Mr Biles used to be very strict with me because his son was often sitting with me and I think he overcompensated for favouritism. One day Mr Biles sent me out of the room for some reason that I have since forgotten (usually pretty trivial), and being bored I tried standing on one leg, fell over grabbing a wall mounted fire extinguisher which went off after it hit the ground. Mr Biles rushed out to see what happened and was hit directly by a spray of chemical foam!"

40	E.Starling & Son, Newsagents
40A	George Wilson, Grocer
40B	Asking & Son, Butchers
98	Hampshire & General Friendly Society, William Hitchens, Local Agent
100	Douglas Clarkson, Grocer

North Side

	Methodist Central Hall & School Room, see Fratton Road
7	Alfred Clements, Potato Merchant
15	Hearts Of Oak Benefit Society, District Office
	In 1923 was Morris Onion and the Co-operative Building Society that later moved to Fratton Road
17	Mrs E.Hollands, Confectioner
51	Walter Harris, Tailor
61	Captain Stewart Williams, Private Enquiry Agent
75	Ronald Lobb, Watch Maker
77	Charles Lewis, Confectioner
145	Ernest Coppard, Fried Fish Shop
	This is still a fish and chip shop but the entrance is in Renny Road.

Purbrook Road, named after the village.
South Side

6	Frederick Timpson, Builder

Renny Road, named after Gunner & Renny Solicitors who dealt with sale of land.
South Side

58	Miss Eileen Mawell-Huggett T.C.L., Teacher of Music
92	Samuel Haysman, Teacher of Music
94	Samuel Haysman, Teacher of Music

North Side

13	Mrs V.Moore, Dressmaker
39	James McElwaine, Grocer
59	Mrs F.Ware, Shopkeeper

Samuel Road Part was started in 1874, in 1889 more building land was for sale, building was complete by 1894. The northern part was known as Union Street.

East Side

"From 1912 to 1943 my home was 25 Samuel Road. The house was reputed to be one of the original houses from the old Union Street and one story credited it with having once been a dairy.

Although a very small house it boasted seven equally small rooms:- three bedrooms upstairs and front, middle and back downstairs plus the scullery. The toilet was at the bottom of the garden. No bathroom just a tin bath in the scullery, in fact I seem to remember getting a better soaking running behind the horse drawn water cart that came around the streets in the dry months wetting the road surface to keep the dust down. We did not own the house but rented it from a Mr Chandler who lived in Fourth Street. He also owned number 23.

Our family consisted of Mum, Dad, my seven older brothers and me. Four of my brothers were in the army and when home on leave had to sleep on the floor - as it was we were sometimes three to a bed. The bedrooms were lit by candles, only downstairs had the luxury of gas lamps.

Our play area was the street - no traffic! The only traffic in Samuel Road consisted of our soapbox carts and the mens' pushbikes and there weren't many of those. We also went to the 'Buttercup and Daisy Fields' (see our book Memories of Over the Lines)off of Langstone Road and to St. Mary's Churchyard. We mainly played around the tombstones and over the 'puddings'. These were probably graves. We usually ended up being chased by a man with a cane, hence the shout 'Here comes old caner'. Whether or not he was the sexton I do not know. I also remember the mass grave and memorial to those who died in the Royal George when she capsized at Spithead. My brothers once played football with a skull found in one of the crumbling vaults. There were plenty of kids in the road and I remember one family with nine children in a two bedroom house!

In Samuel Road was a wall which formed the end of the garden of a shop in Adames Road. The wall had a door which opened onto a pathway which led to two steps leading into the backdoor of the shop. This was Redman, a grocery store cum off-licence. As kids we would use this as a short cut, running through the door which had a bell attached. When the owner came to serve all he would see was a backside disappearing out the front door. The counter ran from front to back of the shop so in order to stop us using this short cut he eventually turned the counter across the shop so blocking our 'run'. A sad note regarding the children at that time was the infant mortality rate. I remember at least four deaths at a very early age.

The adults entertainment seemed to centre around the old Castle Bannerman on the St. Mary's Road corner. 'Comin up the Ma?' was regularly heard. As kids we were naturally not allowed in but I do remember the brewer's dray pulled by two huge carthorses. The landlord was a Mr Geary.

New years' eve would see Mrs Payne over the road get her piano out into the road (I believe it came out through the window) and all the neighbours gathering round for a spot of dancing and a good old sing-song."

Nina Craddock (Née Hartt)

| 53 | Charles Cole, Herbalist |

West Side

36/36A	Rose Cottage 1885
58	Mrs Alice Marchment, Shopkeeper
	Now converted into a house.

Sandringham Road, in 1896 the first house was built by Mr Woods

North Side

1   Dr Theophilus Mead M.R.C.S.Eng, L.S.A.
Dr Kenneth Mead L.R.C.P.
The Mead family were doctors here in the 1890s and for many years after. Other branches of the family practised elsewhere in the city.

5   Herbert Ablitt & Son, Coal and Coke Merchants

7   Maurice Ablitt & Son, Blacksmiths

South Side

Southsea Mineral Water Co., (A. R. Snow & G.J.Nunn) 1902-1921

Southsea Mineral Water Co., (Albert Snow proprietor) 1923-1940

From 1899 to 1901 they were at Somers Road North on the corner with Vivash Road.

Mr Snow lived in a house in Sandringham Road which was named Corona in 1920 until 1930, from then until the war Mrs Arnold lived at Corona. There is no connection with the firm Corona.

Selbourne Terrace   Southsea Mineral Water Co.

2	Lloyds Bank
5	Mill & Dixon, House Agents
8	Mrs Annie Coleman, Apartments
10	Mrs Emily Warren, Apartments
13	Jeram & Co., Coal Merchants. This was Selbourne Villa

Fratton Station

The railway came to Portsmouth in 1847.

Known as Fratton from 1885 to 1905 Fratton & Southsea Station from 1905 to 1921 when it became plain Fratton again.

The new branch line to East Southsea was opened on July 1st 1885.

On 6th August 1914 the branch line to East Southsea was closed "We waited for a troop train arriving at platform 2 in World War 1 with our Union Jacks flying. When the train arrived it was full of German prisoners of war who were marched and carried on stretchers to Fawcett Road School which was used as a hospital."

Sheffield Road, named after the town.

North Side

15	Mrs Mabel Dowse, Midwife
47	Edward Porter, Decorator

| 65 | Dainty Cream Cheese Products Co. (Henry Mott), Biscuit manufacturers |

Thorncroft Road was adopted in 1898

North Side

23	Walter Shott, Builder, plumber, etc.
33	Misses Barton & Willis, Dress Makers
43	Frederick Clark, Decorator

Trafalgar Place, named after the naval battle. In 1808 a row of cottages called Trafalgar Cottages were built at the rear of Fratton Lane. They ran from the rear of the Trafalgar Arms to Sandringham Road. By 1834 the road is marked on the map as Trafalgar Place. On the 1860 map the cottages in Trafalgar Place are shown as Nelson's Cottages. By 1898 the old Trafalgar Place had gone and a new Trafalgar Place was built parallel to the old but further east. By 1904 it was known as Trafalgar Road but it became a place again by 1910. By 1938 most of the houses had gone and were superseded by business premises.

West Side

| 1 | Samuel Knight & Co., Bakers |

"Knight's bakery had their bread ovens and many times I watched the men putting wood faggots in the fire. They also had a bakery and corner shop in Somers Road North. Their bread was super and I had bread from their roundsmen when I married and living further along the road. Mother had them when she lived in Crofton Road, Milton, until they went out of business."

| 7 | J.Littlefield & Co., Blind Makers (Workshop) |

Maternity Hospital & Child Welfare Clinic built at a cost of £11,000 in 1928, Miss Arkoll was the first Matron.

1934	Municipal Maternity Hospital, Matron Miss P.M.Hughes
1937 to 1948	City of Portsmouth Child Welfare Clinic
1951 to 1960	City of Portsmouth Child Welfare Clinic, Portsmouth Chest Clinic, and City Analyst Department
1962 to 1964	City of Portsmouth Child Welfare Clinic, and City Analyst Department
1966 to 1967	City of Portsmouth Child Welfare Clinic, Portsmouth Chest Clinic, and City Analyst Department
1971	City of Portsmouth Maternity & Child Welfare Clinic, City of Portsmouth Medical Social Workers, Portsmouth & District Family Planning Centre, Portsmouth Chest Clinic, City Analyst Department
1973	City of Portsmouth Maternity & Child Welfare Clinic, City of Portsmouth Medical Social Workers, Portsmouth & District Family Planning Centre, City of Portsmouth

1976

Health Visitors, City of Portsmouth District Nurses, City of Portsmouth Health Education Unit
Portsmouth & South East Hants Health District Offices, Health Education Unit, Maternity & Child Welfare Centre, Health Visitors, District Nurses.

The building was boarded up until 1977 when the City Council purchased it from the Health Authority. It was then renovated and in July 1980 Her Majesty the Queen and HRH Prince Philip came to declare the Centre officially open as Fratton Community Centre. The sports hall was opened in 1986 by Princess Diana.

"In 1929 we opened the new maternity hospital. The day before I sent two of my nurses to pick violets and primroses and celandines in the wood at the holt at Horndean. They went by bus, up the hill at Horndean, which was done away with soon after, and brought back a whole lot. It turned out we could put a vase on every locker of these mixed flowers. It was opened, I think by the Lord Mayor. We had no separate rooms, we had a little room where we put the difficult deliveries and they were put there while they were waiting because they needed a little managing. Other than that we had one labour ward which had double glass windows and in those days that was a wonderful thing to have. We had twenty eight beds.

There was one baby which was rather yellow and the matron could not understand it. She asked if it was receiving proper treatment and I Said "Oh, yes, I'm doing it myself matron". So on the third day she said "It's still very grey isn't it?" So I said "Yes, but it is taking its food and putting on weight. I cannot understand it. After Matron had gone downstairs, one of the nurses came and said "Mrs so and so, wants to speak to you". I went straight in and she asked if we were worried about her baby. I said "We were not really worried but we think he's a funny colour." "Oh!" she said "But sister my husband is Chinese!"

In those days women would usually have their first baby in the hospital and then, if there were no complications or problems, they would have their following children at home.

Another reason for having their children in hospital was that the conditions at home were so poor. I remember that one person from Fratton wrote to the paper and said that she thought it was wonderful to have two weeks of such wonderful treatment and good food.

A lot of women had very many children - the largest I ever came across was 21 babies. When I was delivering her, her muscles were very lax and the baby wouldn't come. She said "I'll tell you what to do nurse. When the next pain comes, put your knee on my stomach". I said "I couldn't do that, I'm sure I should be breaking the rules of the Central Midwives Board." "Well it's the only way to get it my dear." she said. So I did and the baby just popped out. So that was all right. The next day I went to see her and she said, "My Husband wants to see you". I thought now there's going to be a good fight about something. I went down to the kitchen. He said "Are you the one who delivered my wife?" I said "Yes". "Well here's a present for you". It was a half pint bottle of stout.

Occasionally I did get called out. Once I went to a very poor part of Portsmouth and the police took me there! They said could someone come to this women as she was in labour and they didn't know what to do. I found this woman on a mattress of iron - the wire kind, with a baby at one end of about two and her in heavy labour at the other end; no pillow, no blankets to cover her or anything. There were eight families living in the same house and one tap for water in the garden. She had her baby and was as well as I was.

Another woman; the door bell rang and they said "sister please come this woman looks rather seedy". I went down and as I got hold of her the baby was born on the doormat. So I collected her together and took her upstairs. When I rang up the medical officer and told him he said "I think we had better call him 'Mat-Hugh'!" and they did indeed call him Matthew.

I was there thirteen years, we had about 300 babies a year as an average during that period. At that time it was the only maternity hospital in Portsmouth. Then after some years we knew that St. Mary's Hospital were building their new building for maternity work and our patients would go there, so I left while they were on the move. I never worked at St. Marys, it was much bigger there they had many patients in a ward, we had nine at most. Small wards are much better, in big wards if one person has trouble they all catch it."

Sister Hughes

East Side

A.Clements, Wholesale Fruiterer (Stores)

North Side

Harry Cowdrey, Motors for hire

Walmer Road

South Side

2	Edmund Hewitt, Grocer
4	Morris & Gallop, Confectioners
14	Fratton's Aircraft Factory "Early in 1947 a builder's yard in Walmer Road came up for sale. The eventual buyers were to become one of the city's larger employers (although not for many years to come) - Hants and Sussex Aviation. This concern had their first premises here, in fact they were paid for on the spot - try that today. Perhaps 'Aircraft Factory' is a bit misleading as at the time all that was being made were the packing crates. These were made in a rather draughty, leaky environment with very little natural light but at that time any premises at all were a god send. Although only packing cases they were for delicate equipment and actually had to be protected for transit. The only packing available at reasonable cost was wood shavings from the city timberyards. The crates were packed in a railway container for their journey to Edinburgh and each container needed a lorry load of shavings. These were hand packed and naturally a lot of shavings found their way into Walmer Road and were blown everywhere. To avoid the wrath of the road's housewives we had to literally sweep the street after every consignment had been packed. During this period the staff numbered about twenty-five persons and as well as making packing cases we managed to design a small aircraft. Although this was eventually built it had to wait until we moved to the City Airport in 1949 when the Walmer Road premises, including the flat above the entrance were sold." Mr E. Hawes
184	Portham & Co., Blind Makers

North Side

55A	Joseph Manning, Grocer
99	Frederick Church, Baker
157	Ernest Rogers, Decorator

Woodland Street

East Side

5	Edgar Palmer, pianoforte tuner

West Side

12	George Seymour & Son, Marine Store Dealers

The following roads were residential only Ethel Road, Forton Road

This booklet was compiled by the members of the W.E.A. Local History Group which meets at the North End Adult Learning Centre, Derby Road, North End. The group is made up of local people who wish to record the history of ordinary peoples' lives and the streets in which they live. The group is very informal and welcomes new members who care to come to Derby Road on a Tuesday evening during term time or write to us.

Class Members:
> Leonard Bufton, Anton Cox, Frank Deacon, Peter Eaves, Betty Fowkes, Peter Galvin, Malcolm Garlick, Ann Gilbert, Kevin Goldring, Pat Goldring, Charles Hutchins, Alan Jenking, Stephen Pomeroy (Chairman & Editor), Chris Redgrave, Frank and Jean Scott, Jeff Smith, Rita Wall, Margaret Webster (Treasurer).

Honorary Members:
> Don Miles (Typesetting).
> Olive Cook (Proofreader)

Affiliated Members:
> Des Beaumont, Morecambe, Lancashire
> Vic Burly, Brisbane, Australia
> Roger Cook, Kingslake West, Australia
> Maggie Munro, Frankstone, Australia

Contributors:

> Keith Barnard, Mr. H. Barnett, Mr. M. Constad, Mrs. Nina Craddock (née Hartt), Gron Evans, Mr. Val Fontana, Ken Hampton, Mr. E. Hawes, Miss Hughes, Mrs. M. McBride, Mrs. E. Pratt (née Allen), Ron, Fratton Community Association.

References:

> Portsmouth Evening News.
> Portsmouth Records Office, William Tarring Papers.

First published in 1997.
Reprinted 2001.